FENNEC FOX

BY TYLER GRADY

Dylanna Press

Fennec foxes are **mammals** that are native to the deserts of northern Africa. They can be found across the Sahara Desert and the Sinai and Arabian peninsulas.

They are related to dogs, wolves, and other types of foxes. Their scientific name is *Vulpes zerda*, which means small fox.

They are the national animal of Algeria.

---

mammals – warm-blooded animals with hair or fur that give birth to live young

6

The smallest members of the Canidae family, they weigh between 1½ to 3½ pounds (.68-1.58 kg) and average 9 to 16 inches (23-40 cm) in length. Their tails are about 8 inches (20 cm) long.

A distinctive feature of the fennec fox is their large ears. Compared to their tiny faces and small pointed snouts, their ears are huge, measuring 4 to 6 inches (10-15 cm). The large surface area helps to cool them off in the desert heat.

Fennec foxes live in deserts and experience both extremely hot and cold temperatures.

Their thick fur and bushy tail allow them to stay warm on cold desert nights while also protecting and **insulating** them from the hot sun.

Another way fennec foxes beat the desert heat is through **panting**. Panting helps to lower their body temperature in times of extreme heat by exhaling hot air from the lungs.

_____

insulation – material that reduces transfer of heat

panting – breathing with short, quick breaths

The fennec fox has many physical **adaptations** to its environment.

Their pale sand-colored fur acts as camouflage, allowing them to blend in with their desert home. The light color also helps to reflect the sun.

Their paws have an extra layer of fur on the bottom that provides traction for them to run on the desert sand while also protecting them from burning.

As mentioned, their large ears also help them keep their cool by radiating body heat.

_____

adaptations – ways in which a species becomes fitted into its natural environment to increase its chance of survival

Fennec foxes are **omnivores**.

Their diet consists largely of insects including locusts and grasshoppers. They also eat small rodents, lizards, bird eggs and some fruit, leaves, and roots.

One unique adaptation to their desert environment is their ability to live without drinking water. They are able to get enough fluids from the foods they eat. Their kidneys are able to retain water for long periods of time.

---

omnivore – an animal that eats both meat and plants

13

Fennec foxes hunt alone and at night.

Their large ears enable them to listen to **prey** underneath the desert sand. They will then quickly dig down in the sand to catch their target.

Despite their small size they are able to jump up to 2 feet (.6 meters) in the air and can spring quickly upon their prey.

They will store, or **cache** extra food for future use.

.
_____

prey – animal that is hunted by another animal for food

cache – food that is hidden and stored for future use

Fennec foxes are **monogamous**

and a pair will usually mate for life. Breeding season takes place in January and February and they give birth in the spring. Pregnancy lasts about 50 days.

Fennec fox babies are called kits. A mother fox will give birth once a year to between 2-5 kits. They are blind and helpless when born but grow up quickly, reaching adulthood around 9 months.

Both parents will help to raise the baby foxes. The mother fox stays in the den with the kits while the father fox hunts for food and protects them.

---

monogamous – to have only one mate; a bonded pair

Fennec foxes spend most of the day asleep in underground burrows in the sand. This helps them avoid the hot sun and extreme heat of the desert. These dens are usually around 3 feet below ground.

They are **nocturnal** and can see very well in the dark. They normally don't come out of their dens until around dusk to search for food.

They are **territorial** and use urine and feces to mark their territory.

---

nocturnal – an animal that is most active at night

territorial – an animal that occupies and defends a specific area

Fennec foxes are social animals.

The live in groups of up to ten family members including a breeding pair and their offspring, sometimes from several litters.

A male fox is called a reynard and a female is called a vixen. A group of fennec foxes is called a skulk.

Different families of foxes often live close together, building tunnels between their underground dens.

Like other members of the Canidae family, fennec foxes have a complex communication system.

They are very playful animals and they use a variety of **vocalizations** include barking, whimpering, shrieking, growling, and squeaking to communicate and establish social rank.

When startled, they can give off a musky scent, similar to a skunk.

---

vocalization – the sounds an animal makes

The average lifespan of a fennec fox is ten years in the wild. They can live up to sixteen years in captivity.

The total population is not known but they are not considered to be an **endangered species**.

---

endangered species – a species that is danger of becoming extinct

Due to their small size, fennec foxes are often prey to other larger animals. Owls often hunt baby foxes, and hyenas, jackals, and caracals prey on them as well.

However, fennec foxes are extremely alert and very fast and are often able to **out-maneuver** predators.

Another threat to fennec foxes is humans. They are hunted for their fur and also trapped to be sold as pets.

In addition, increased human settlement into their traditional territories has led to habitat loss.

_____

outmaneuver – to evade by moving faster or with better agility

Fennec foxes are becoming increasingly popular as exotic house pets.

There is a large market for fennec foxes as pets and many are captured for that reason. Commercial breeders are also raising foxes for this purpose.

However, they are wild animals and do not make good house pets. They are easily startled and do not like loud noises.

In addition, because of their strong digging **instinct**, they can be quite destructive indoors.

_____

instinct – a strong natural behavior or ability

Fennec foxes are beautiful and fascinating animals. They are well-adapted to surviving in their native harsh desert climate.

Although they may look like cute pets, they should be respected and protected as wild creatures.

Word Search

```
T H G N O M N I V O R E S F P
G U U J L D D G B H M U A E C
D K R P J S N E J A O Q D N L
U I V U N I P B S M T C A N I
U T K Y T O P E A E D Z P E F
G S X N L W C G C K R Z T C E
T N U N J W O T Q I X T A W S
G H J P O N T I U T E K T F P
D W P R O G M A O R R S I N A
J Q R M J N Q G D Q N A O E N
D U H Y S L A M M A M A N I R
B K L U K S T A E H L Y L S N
P R E Y L H A B I T A T R M T
L E G A L F U O M A C I D B H
H C C R M P R E D A T O R X E
```

ADAPTATION	HEAT	NOCTURNAL
BURROW	HUNTING	OMNIVORE
CAMOUFLAGE	KITS	PREDATOR
DESERT	LIFESPAN	PREY
FENNEC	MAMMALS	SKULK
HABITAT	MONOGAMOUS	SPECIES

32

INDEX

Published by Dylanna Press an imprint of Dylanna Publishing, Inc.
Copyright © 2021 by Dylanna Press
Author: Tyler Grady

Printed in the U.S.A.

Made in the USA
Las Vegas, NV
14 November 2021

34456154R00021